Milk, Mess, & Magic

Poems on Parenting

Milk, Mess, & Magic

Poems on Parenting

by

Hannah Seelman

Cover design by Shay Culligan
Cover image by Mae Mu on Unsplash
Author photo by Hannah Seelman

ISBN: 979-8-90146-813-5
Library of Congress Control Number: 2026931903

Kelsay Books
502 South 1040 East, A-119
American Fork, Utah 84003
Kelsaybooks.com

In her debut poetry collection, Hannah Seelman confronts the taboo: that even the most devoted parents sometimes find their children to be tiny, terrible creatures. This is not a collection of blissful poems, nor is it a guide that promotes the best parenting practices . . . it's a story speaking towards the quiet rage, sleepless nights, and the moments of pure love that define the real life of a parent.

For anyone who's ever whispered *I love you*
through clenched teeth—this book is for you.

Acknowledgments

Thank you to the following publications, in which versions of these poems previously appeared:

Ink Nest: "Untitled"
Wingless Dreamer: "Dandelion Neighbors"

This collection would not exist without the support of many individuals.

To my husband Nick, thank you for your encouragement, and reminding me that I can accomplish my dream of writing a book.

To my daughter, thank you for your patience while I was writing this book. You are absolutely precious to me.

To my readers from the past, present, and future, thank you for making space for my words in your life. Receiving an audience to read my words is the biggest reward imaginable.

To families I personally know and have observed, thank you for being my inspiration.

To my Western Michigan University MFA peers and professors, thank you for your feedback and guidance. Your talent is incredible and I've learned so much from you all.

And finally, special thanks to my dog who sits on my lap in the evening while I write. She is an incredible writing buddy and a quality lap warmer.

Contents

More Praise for the Work

I keep returning to the word *aviary* throughout Hannah Seelman's *Milk, Mess, & Magic,* as her poems have an Audubon Society-like splendor. Beyond that, *aviary* evokes a gathering place where nest-nursery is pathway, Seelman's aesthetic one of "tender vibrance."

This collection's dragons and unicorns are side by side with maternal selflessness, the kingfishers hovering. "Carry On," my favorite poem, features a speaker who buys a birdbath for a mother robin because "[s]he looks up at the awning in exasperation." The wingspan is empathy to simpatico.

The author's observational gifts are in the same company as Carmen Giménez and Aimee Nezhukumatathil, a daughter's "honey eyes / sparking when lightning cracks."

—Jon Riccio, author of *Agoreography*
and *The Orchid in Lieu of a Horse*

I.
Weight of Wings

New Reflection

A month ago I was in
love with my own reflection,
not knowing the full
sacrifice of being selfless
until I held such a small
heart in my arms.

Somedays

I am the bleak sky and cold,
self-doubt is responsible
for my shivering.

My chest shudders,
Can I even do this?
I dread when my baby wakes up,
and only want to scroll TikTok for hours.

But I'm having lunch with friends today,
so I pack up baby,
slap on a jack-o'-lantern face,

and I laugh,
and I look fresh,
and I say my baby is bliss
and all my friends say the same about theirs.

After lunch we hug then go back home,
where loneliness resides beside doubt,
and our freezing hearts cry.

We could be a blanket for one another,
but we're too damn
proud to admit
we're cold.

Growing Pains

I hate the feeling of milk in my breasts,
but I'm told formula isn't as healthy.

I'm running on four hours of sleep,
and even gallons of caffeine won't perk me up.

I only cry in pillows or the shower,
because I don't want my husband to hear me.

This morning I lost my phone,
and found it in the refrigerator.

I need a few minutes to compose myself,
but I can't leave my baby without my soul screaming.

I see myself in the window's reflection,
but don't see the same face as before.

I'm suffering but no one wants to see,
how a mother could be anything but blissful.

Lullaby

I tried everything to get you to sleep. Even the owls called out, marveling at your stubbornness. I sang every lullaby imaginable—"Twinkle Twinkle," "Hushabye Baby," "Rockabye Baby"—each one tumbling from my lips only to bounce off your flushed red ears. They always turn that color when you're angry—just like my sister's.

Tears slowly traced their way down my cheeks as the owls called once more. I closed my eyes in frustration and despair—what kind of parent can't get their own baby to sleep? Then, as if summoned by a lyrical angel, a different song came to mind. Desperation turned to recklessness, and I began to sing—Salt-N-Pepa's "Push It."

Sassy words and playful beats spilled from my talentless mouth, my voice embracing the absurdity. As I half-laughed through the lyrics, I glanced down. And couldn't believe it: you were asleep.

Confessions

Confession #1
I always love my baby but sometimes don't like her.

Confession #2
Watching my strong husband fall apart during our baby's first year was the hardest thing I've ever endured.

Confession #3
What if I'm not good enough for her?

Confession #4
I use my baby as an excuse to leave social events early—and I don't feel bad about it.

Confession #5
I chose to stay sober after giving birth. I was afraid that if I started drinking, I wouldn't stop.

Confession #6
I dread brushing my daughter's hair because her screams could shatter stone.

Confession #7
I crave quiet time, but when I finally get it, guilt creeps in.

Confession #8

I check on my baby in the middle of the night, paranoid she might be cold . . . or dead.

Confession #9

Expensive baby clothes are ridiculous. Best case, they grow out of them in months. Worse case, they stain them on day one.

Confession #10

I feel like I'm not doing a good job despite being told otherwise—I don't believe them.

Calling the Fire Department

All of a sudden, my home fell silent.

My niece and nephew were over for a playdate.
They went to my daughter's room to play with dinosaurs.
For the last two hours, the kids had been shouting.
Now—nothing.

At first, I wondered if they had solved their own problems,
maybe even settled into a board game together.
If so, maybe I could read a book?

I hadn't finished one in years.

Finally, I called out, *What are you guys doing?*

Nothing but soft, frantic voices.

I've heard whispers like this before—the kind that come
when kids know they're about to be caught.
The last time, it had been a jack-o'-lantern
stuck on my nephew's head.

I closed my eyes, listening intently.

There was a loud *thump.*
Followed by complete silence.

Shit. This can't be good.

I knew this quiet too well—it meant a plan was unraveling,
a scheme falling apart.

I speed-walked to my daughter's bedroom,
half not wanting to know the situation.
I twisted the metal handle and found my child and her cousin
standing frozen with wide eyes.

Where is the third?

A giggle.

In the corner, my two-year-old niece dangled upside down,
her right foot woven between two steps of a plastic slide.
A small bat and a bottle of glue sat on the ground—evidence
of a desperate, failing rescue mission.

My nephew and daughter were trying to break the steps by force
and glue them back together.

Jesus. They could have broken her foot.

Her ankle had already begun to swell.
Peanut butter, oil—useless.
The circulation was cutting off too fast
and sawing off the steps would be too dangerous.

No other options.

I called 911.

Minutes later, sirens swirled down my street
like a blue and red tornado.
As the fire truck pulled up, I glanced outside—
the sun angled through crisp clouds,
casting a tender vibrance over my flower garden.
This year, it looked obscenely gorgeous.

One glorious day, I'll put a hammock chair out there
and just sit for hours reading a true crime novel or better yet
a relaxing book of poems.

Big Emotions

I wanted to punch a kid today.
Right in the throat.
I didn't, though.

My daughter said hi enthusiastically
as he went down the slide.
He ignored her—or maybe he
didn't hear her—before trotting off.

My daughter's face dulled sadly,
a bit of glimmer lost,
but soon reignited as a butterfly
rested on a nearby daisy,
yellow wings pulsing in black patterns.
A monarch—her favorite.

I almost committed a crime today.
But I stopped myself.
Barely.

Bias

My nephew handed me his drawing, expecting my praise. I glanced down, trying to make sense of the chaos. It was clusters of scribbles tangled with jagged shapes, as if a poltergeist had possessed his crayons. My first thought? *What the actual hell am I looking at?* A square sat on the end of a stick, attached to a large oval mass. Black smudges scattered across the page, not confined to the mysterious blob but smeared haphazardly throughout. It was nothing special, just a typical kid's drawing, the kind that parents stack up and end up throwing out. He told me it was an elephant swimming in a pool with a toy car. I nodded. Of course it was.

Shortly after my daughter handed me her picture, and my first thought was: *Holy shit she's a goddamn prodigy.* With a little guidance from the artist, I took in the details of her magnificent work. She had drawn a blue and purple cheetah which was wearing a top hat and sunglasses. It was either mid-sprint or sitting on a toilet. I asked her for clarification, but she refused to commit, leaving it up to my own interpretation. Just as cleverly she shaded the sky not only blue but sections of red and black creating a unique tone of play paired with apprehension. My child didn't just draw; she dominated and to celebrate we left the family reunion early to get ice cream.

Mommy Helpers

Grandma = Mommy

Grandpa = Mommy

Daddy = Mommy

Puppy = Mommy

Teacher = Mommy

Her Friend's Mom = Mommy

Aunt = Mommy

Uncle = Mommy

My Friend = Mommy

My Friend's Mom = Mommy

My Friend's Dog = Mommy

Neighbors = Mommies

Actual Mommy = Bird

Never Change

This morning, Gabi wanted a yellow marker.
We were coloring pictures of sunflowers.
I took the cap off for her.
She wanted to do it herself.
She proceeded
to chuck the marker at my face.

She is such a bitch.

Tbf most toddlers are.
They're self centered and brutal.
But my child is bolder than her friends . . .
She speaks/screams her mind,
approaches strangers with confidence,
sings as if the world should bow down to her.

A medium stopped my daughter and I.
We were shopping at TJ-Maxx.
She informed me my daughter is
very strong and one day; powerful.
Then she just walked away.

Jesus Christ, more powerful?

Gabi enjoys plucking petals off my tulips.
I tell her not to.
I'm given a look that says "fuck the police."

Making eye contact,
she continues peeling off petals,
I end up hauling her away as she bites my chest.

A toddler is my abuser.

In the spring we went to a park with a rockwall.
It was for kids over twice her age.
Her determination said otherwise.
She made it. Her face triumphant—
an expression of fire
that can't be extinguished.

We go to parks constantly now,
because she wants to kiss danger
while climbing even higher than before.
I spot her, but she's never fallen.

I'll always spot her anyway.

Unicorn

At home, my daughter is a baby unicorn—
radiant, gentle, full of affection.

But when the stars align and hunger takes hold,
she transforms into a full-grown unicorn,
her sharpened horn a subtle warning.
She's still endearing, yet slightly formidable.

When exhaustion collides with hunger,
she remains a unicorn,
but now the daggered horn pairs with slick talons.

If hunger, fatigue, *and* thirst intertwine?
She becomes a restless creature,
summoned from another realm,
stands dagger-horned, knife-taloned, foaming at the mouth.

Robin Nest

The robin's nest outside the window
has two yellow triangle beaks
whose high pitched croaks
scream for food.
My own baby sits in her highchair
also screeching in hunger.

I watch as mama bird flies back
with worms which
the babies accept.
I hand my baby a strawberry,
pristine in ruby and velvet touch.
She throws it on the floor.

Papa bird flies back with blackberries and his babies
inhale them.
I cut apples and sprinkle them with cinnamon.
My daughter bites them while laughing,
bulleting me with a cloud of half chewed bits.

Gabrielle, I say pointing to the window, *look*
how the baby birds are eating so nicely.
Those tiny beaks don't spit anything out!

My daughter pauses, sits locking eyes
on the birds, and then back to me.
With a baby bird shriek
she looks up, her mouth unnaturally wide.
I drop a spoonful of yogurt into her mouth, she swallows,
smiles and then becomes a baby bird again and again.

Garden Day

She sprinkles daisy petals
into a kiddie pool—
rainwater and bugs swirling below.
Pauses.
Lowers his face.

No, don't drink it!

Grabs my hose,
"sneaks" up behind me.
I fake surprise
as cold water splashes my leg.

Oh, you got me!

Finds a toad beneath the
dewy rose bush,
slowly lifts it to her lips.

No, don't kiss it!

Follows a bumblebee,
clumsily landing on a flower,
reaches to pet the fuzzy bumble.

Holy shit, don't touch those ones!

Shimmering Notes

The first time *mama*
  came from your lips,
  the sun beamed in a song
    I haven't heard in years.
  And when the shimmering notes
        flooded within me,
                I couldn't help but smile.

Catching Dragon, Part 1

I did not expect to see a tumbling mass
crudely falling from the sky,
that my youngest daughter
would drop her sidewalk chalk and run
across the yard to catch it before hitting the lawn.
She held that feeble baby dragon cupped in her palm,
while it hid his aqua and gold gemmed face beneath her right thumb.

After not finding a single adult dragon lurking anywhere,
she decided to adopt the baby.
So she brought him inside,
sat on the couch comforting him.

It's okay little buddy. I'll make you feel better.

She built him a blanket nest,
he gave a soft growl as he laid down,
smoke gently curling from his nostrils.

As I watched her stroke his brow,
I wondered what it would feel like
to be born with such a full heart-
that when a dragon falls from the heavens,
one would become his mother
without needing a single question answered.

II.
Wild and Worn

Mirror Baby

The minute of my life when I saw that strange baby—
glossy-eyed, squishy-skinned,
her face twisting between terrible screams—
I felt something shift.

It's fascinating how quickly,
how willingly,
I changed my definition of beautiful.

Balanced Sky

I never knew I was missing a moon—
until one night, rocking my baby,
beneath its glow.
Her eyes locked on mine, dazzling.
There and then, I decided to
be a sun for her.

And I made—
my soul tender as tulips.
my voice gentle as dusk.
my heart steady as morning light.

And I found the fullness of a quiet moon.

Carry On

The robin nesting on the front porch light is a new mother,
and it's nice—because we can be stressed out together.

I can tell she's new; her feathers ruffled on her back,
much like my forever-tangled hair.

She feeds her chicks,
flutters off to a nearby pine branch,
standing perfectly still,
staring into the abyss.

The father robin isn't a slacker by any means,
bringing worms and caterpillars in endless supply.
But the chicks cling to their mother,
screeching obscenely until she returns.

Then—calmed beneath her feathers—
they begin roughhousing, hungry.
Hangry, even.

She looks up at the awning in exasperation
before flying off.
I get it.

This morning it was raining,
and judging by their ungodly sirens,
the babies *hated* it.

My baby did too—
for some reason
rain pattering on the roof
irks her.

I pressed my forehead
against the window,
and sighed.

As mama bird settled on her chicks,
she gave me a side glance.
Her beady eye
met my blue—understanding.

This afternoon,
I bought a birdbath,
placed it close enough so she can see the nest,
but far enough away
where her chick's calls
aren't as piercing.

Within half an hour,
she was fluffing her feathers,
splashing in the cool water,
letting herself breathe.

I sipped my coffee,
sinking into the chair,
Thanking Christ for a moment of quiet—

The chicks
began shrieking again.
My baby
started wailing.

Mama robin slowly flew to her nest.
I begrudgingly turned to the baby.

And we carried on.

Curled Lamb

My baby will not come from my womb,
but my heart.

Today,
she is a curled lamb,
softly stirring between my pulses.

I feel, but can not hold her.

But tomorrow,
God will shepherd her
into my arms.

And baby will sleep
on my chest,
head nuzzled against my skin,
her breath soft as wool.

Owls Watching

On which breath will I taste wild?
Mother possums carry kits on back,
wolves grab puppy scruffs between gentle jaws,
owls nestle within oak.

I open my eyes to moon
breath glowing from above,
I must have waited a long time.

Baby sleeps
inhaling sweetly
her tiny body smells my skin,
eyes echoing love
behind thin lids.

I cradle her in the meadow
amongst the fireflies.
Oh dear wild!

Moss cushions
beneath my bare feet,
summer air lingers
against bristled tongue.

Baby stirs her
cheek against my chest.
owls watching—
I too am now
blessed in a mother's
world.

Changed Stars

Have you seen the stars tonight?
I've never seen so many glistening above.
They're singing light as I rock baby—
her lashes flickering in dreams.

What has become of those unruly gems?
Look how they spark and pulse as hearts—
breathing light into my chest.

The Spring My Child Fell in Love with Geese

Last year, I despised geese—
dirty, aggressive, noisy, pesky.
Always shitting everywhere,
waiting for bare feet to squish.

But have you seen them this year?
Their slick feathers, smooth as pearls,
their necks more elegant than swans.

They guard their goslings—
bravely honking, wings expanding like a butterfly's,
exposing hearts to shield their fluff babies.

My daughter adores all geese.
When she spots a flock, her face blooms like a sunflower.
She claps, waves, and chimes,
Hello, geese friends! How are you today?
I even give a slight wave.

The geese look at us like we're idiots,
swim away in annoyance.
My daughter blows kisses and shouts,
Bye-bye, geese! See ya later!
before clutching my hand,
leading me toward another flock.

Sipping Tea

After Rudy Francisco

I once enjoyed self-love
the same way I drank tea.

I used to not drink it.

Whenever I did, it tasted bitter,
something wrong—
nothing like berries on the packaging.
False advertising.

But one day, Gabi was brushing/tangling my hair,
and she called me her *beautiful mommy.*

So, I tried tea again—
a raspberry blend.
And learned to sip slowly, taste sweetness,
and finally, found warmth settle inside me.

Finding My Daughter

One day I asked the leafy oak
Why? She only rustled and told me to ask the wise ocean.

I shouted to rumbling ocean
Why? She exhaled waves rolling to shore and said maybe an owl
will know.

To the Owl, I cried
Why? Her eyes widened and told me she didn't know either before
she flew into the stars.

Disheartened in the morning,
my daughter and I walked to the lake.
When the smooth water came into view, she ran.
I reached the bank shortly after
and sat on the wooden dock watching
sparrows cruise across water,
their soft bellies inches off the surface.

Before I could even question the water,
ask her *why would a god take away a mother's child,*
she whispered warmth that said
no one can really know for sure,
and that she feels two sets of children's
feet splashing, two voices laughing, two hearts pounding.

A breeze kissed my cheek and I felt my daughter's wings.
Sun rays glimmered her halo.
Tears still spilled from my eyes.

My soul still throbbed
but my chest was beating,
and like the lightness of clouds,
I ran into the water and played.

Catching Dragon, Part 2

I didn't realize a shimmery plated
dragon lizard couldn't fly immediately.
That ours could only flutter a few
inches off the ground before collapsing.

That the baby dragon was actually
quite fast on his clawed feet,
zooming around with his webbed
wings trailing behind him like two
mini flags as he and my daughters played chase.

The baby dragon peed
on the floor and in a panic set my shoes
on fire and while I put a glass of water on
my doomed Nike's, the dragon's wide eyes
began to swell into slow tears that dripped
off his inky lashes.

My youngest instantly swooped him up and
gave him kisses before pouring him a bubble
bath. He used his bat-like wings to paddle
around the tub as my daughter sang *Rubber Ducky*
and blew suds off her palms,
shimmering opal onto baby dragon's armored nose.

Privacy

While pregnant, I swore: no bathroom trips with an audience.

Privacy was sacred.

Now three years in,
I'm belting *Old MacDonald* with my daughter . . .
who is sitting on my lap
while I pee.

Gray Stone

Last week my child turned into a sparrow
She graced sky with her elegant tricks,
twirled in clouds,
rested on oaks,
raced Canadian geese in flight.

She could have flown
anywhere, but she landed,
grabbed my hand,
pointed to a small robin
hopping in the grass.
She shouted, *how beautiful!*

In early morning she
loves to dive into Lake Michigan.
Like a kingfisher at dawn she
mixes the sunrise water
on impact-swirling rainbows,
then resurfaces with laughter.

She's teaching me
how to be a sparrow.
To be weightless and
taste the wind singing,
To never need the ground.
One day I'll see robins
and name them *incredible.*

Hand and Claw

Why is the nape of her neck so precious?
Just above soft shoulder blades,
the place where wolves and lions
carry their young in gentle jaws.

I clutch my child like a possum,
her warmth nestled close,
wrestle softly as a bobcat with cub,
coo as a songbird easing chicks.

My little one chirps,
pounces on my back,
clings to me, unwavering.

Her moonlit eyes,
pull me closer—
both hand and claw.

Why I Watch Dawn

Purple martins drink the morning light,
orange and red reflected over Lake Michigan,
calling their anthem as the sunrise climbs.

Cool fog drifts through pines,
gliding over stone,
rolling to meet the sand and water,
so still—barely stirring until

mother deer and her fawn
push through the clouds, bending
their necks to drink the lake,
while hymns rise from morning doves
calling beneath the spruce.

But mostly, I watch dawn
because my toddler wakes early—
wanting water, applesauce, hugs,
(literally anything to make me wake up)
and to see the deer visit.
At 5:00 AM. Every single morning.

More Confessions

Confession #11

I pour way too much bubble bath into the tub—because if we're doing bubbles, we're doing bubbles.

Confession #12

I never tell my child to use a "quiet voice." I want her to always speak with confidence.

Confession #13

I secretly admire her bravery when she does something she knows I won't approve of.

Confession #14

Sometimes, I cry in the bathroom because my daughter is being difficult.

Confession #15

I can no longer watch true crime documentaries that involve children.

Confession #16

I'm relieved the newborn stage is over, but I never want the toddler stage to end.

Confession #17

I dread my child becoming a teenager—because one day, she'll say something that cuts too deep.

Confession #18

Sometimes, I feel like a terrible person for bringing a child into a world that's falling apart.

Confession #19

I don't really like my friends' kids.

Confession #20

Mental illness is hereditary, and I don't know how I'll face the guilt if she inherits it.

Steady Unicorn

A paved path cruises through a forest,
sun pushes through the thick roof of branches
shimmering red/orange leaves fall as lazy rain drops
falling on a child's pig tails
hand outstretched
an open palm with sharp half eaten acorns
waiting patiently. Her pudgy lips calling as if to a dog,

Come here unicorn! It's okay!

Her older cousin exhales roughly.

We have to go now. It's been 45 minutes and we've moved 6 feet.
I don't think the unicorns are hungry today, okay? I'm bored,
let's just go.

But the girl only shakes her head, pigtails swooshing,
posture unmoving—still as dawn.

More leaves slowly fall, color parachutes swaying down.
Exasperated the oldest closes his eyes and groans only to
open them abruptly—movement in the woods.

Slowly a stout horse glistening between the oaks and pine comes
out from the shadows. His hooves crack twigs and underbrush
while cautiously approaching the little girl.
His spiral horn sharp as knives bows down as he eats the offering
from the small child's
hand while she hums soothingly.

Pine branches begin to sway as a small snort makes the unicorn turn, grumbling into the quiet.

Oh, look—a baby unicorn! Come here little baby, it's okay; your daddy is here!

Tentative as a fawn, a unicorn with a midnight coat stands from her soft pine needle bed under wide spruce branches. Her mane beams in light as stars rain their glimmers to earth. She joins her father and eats slender twigs the little girl is now offering.

It tickles! Her nose has whiskers!

The older cousin plucks a few wild berries from a bush, outstretches a trembling hand.The baby muffles up the berries slowly, nudges his wrist for more and in softness the boy remembers magic.

So Much Depends Upon

After William Carlos William

The kid sized paint brush
drenched in thick blue
placed on soggy paper.

The "washable" paints
poured onto the floor
by sly hands and quick feet.

The brown dogs barking
paws covered in purple
eyeing the brand new couch.

The laundry machine
holding rainbow clothes
dial set on heavy.

The irate toddler
dripping bright paint
with one foot in the tub.

Week 1: My Daughter's Favorite Flower

Dandelion stained fingers hand
me a sunshine bouquet
before turning around
to clasp her thick green watering can.
She walks past roses
straight back to the dandelion patch
which has grown as thick and unshakeable
as a tortoise shell.
Water glimmers down from a dented spout.
Waterfall shadows fall on grass as the weeds drink.
The wind blows seed fluff
soft as white chick feathers.

Week 2: Blowing Dandelion Fluff

She pushes a sticky stem
my way.
I give a big "pufffff"
She claps and screams .
Her eyes bright as lightning

Week 3: Dandelion Mornings

Now we blow dandelion
seeds for nearly an hour
every morning before eating pancakes.

Week 4: Dandelion Rays

My lawn is a full sun,
stretching dandy rays
across surrounding yards—
thick green slowly becoming golden
petaled.

Week 5: Suburban Dandie Yard

In a sea made of lush
rectangles
lives an island
made of white.
Where a child makes
fluff angels
and her mother kicks seeds
in the breeze watching
them parachute away.

Catching Dragon, Part 3

It's not surprising baby dragon
pulled a *Clifford the Big Red Dog*
and quickly outgrew our house.

That the baby dragon was grew so quickly that adjustments
needed to be made before our home collapsed
from his wind-strong movements.

Baby dragon outgrew my daughter's bed
so he slept beside it on the floral printed rug,
but eventually he could barely fit in doorways
and his tail unintentionally
swatted the walls to bits as he wagged
the gemmed spikes whenever he was excited.

So, I built him a ginormous dragon house
which is really a bed enclosed by a shingled roof and
three walls, the fourth being the outside of our home
so through the window he can lay his head on my daughter's bed.

Catching Their Daughter

My niece's greatest magic
is the fire in her tiny chest,
when climbing the park's twisty slide,
slick with morning rain.

She white-knuckle grips the sides,
slips a few feet—tries again.
Teeth grit, breath held,
fingers falter, she slides down—tries again.

Her determined eyes spark,
resilient face burns,
until finally she makes it—
victorious shrieks
fly from her mighty lungs.

But the best part of her magic
is how my heart swells
when she does an impromptu trust fall
off the top.

Serene eyes closed,
eagle arms wide,
she tips back, slowly,
without a single doubt
her dads will catch her.

Wolf-Eyed

Look at the wolves running in her eyes.
Look how their claws press off sharp rock—
leaping/soaring.

They are beautiful.
They are holy.
But sometimes they are too much.

Pay attention to the wolves—
sprinting through forests, playfully rolling on gray/black backs.
They are elegant and freeing and sacred.

Yet sometimes, you want to tame their wild ways,
to make them sit and stay.

But you don't. Because even when they're uncontrolled,
and you're frustrated to tired tears,

you know if endured
your wolf-eyed daughter
will lead packs—howling.

III.
Howl and Hold

Palm Reading

Mediums say palm lines
whisper glimpses into
marriage
children
finances
death.

I'm not
on your palm
(mothers never are)
and if so, I've failed.
But you mark mine.

Take my hand, child,
lace your crystal
prints onto my threaded
palm sparking stories.

We are bound,
ribbon veins twisting,
spilling DNA and fortunes.
Fate is already written.
You are already here.

But to make sure,
take your tiny nails,
sharpened lightning,
engrave yourself again
over my soft palm.

While I kiss skyward,
lips trembling in rain,
thanking Christ for
faith
and lust.

Lily Potter's Sacrifice

Originally I thought
a mother's love is the
same as any love; but
since birthing my baby
fire pounds within me.

I have a mindlessness
to die for my child;
not needing
a split second of breath
before acting.

Defending her
would be natural
like flight under sparrow wings
like falling leaves from autumn maples.
like jumping in front of *Avada Kedavra* into a flash of green.

A New Kind of Strength

I thought I was fire
before her birth,
that heat was the only
form of strength.

But I’ve learned
I’m also cool waves
capable of putting
out any flame.

Confessions Unabated

Confession #21

My daughter and I snuggle in her bed, noses pressed together, until she falls asleep.

Confession #22

Every night, I tell her she's smart, strong, brave, kind, and loved—because deep down, that's what I need to hear about myself.

Confession #23

I enjoy the zoo more than my child does.

Confession #24

I can't help but laugh when my daughter swears

Confession #25

I don't actually care if my daughter swears.

Confession #26

I wrote this book to remind parents that parenting is good work—but hard work.

Confession #27

Watching my child grow older means I am too—and that freaks me out.

Confession #28

I only go out to eat with my daughter, because I love watching her say hi to every table like she owns the place.

Confession #29

Every birthday is proof that another year has passed,
and my daughter is still smart, strong, brave, and kind.
She is growing, she is loved, and she knows it.

Confession #30

I have so many more confessions.

He Once Said

Women need to breastfeed, but they also need to make sure
to cover up.
It's not that hard to bounce back after having a baby so long
as they try hard enough.
Until they do bounce back, it's probably best they stay away
from bikinis.

So, now it's my hobby
to lounge in his favorite chair,
wearing only a sports bra—
making sure stretch marks are fully exposed.

And I'll whip out the boobie
feed my child,
and stare him in the eyes,
while slowly sipping sangria.

I wait for him to take the bait,
ready to shred him to bits,
but he never bites—
just leaves the room, frowning.

You see, he's
seen my wild eyes,
heightened senses, and mama-cat strength for days.
He knows I've earned these goddamn tiger stripes
etched onto my belly, breasts, and thighs.

And I am really hungry
waiting to pounce.

To Those with Sons

I hope when “Let It Go” pops up on Spotify,
you don’t tell him to change the song,
but dance alongside him in the family room.

And when he chooses “girl clothes”
instead of truck shirts,
you say he looks super cool
in his sunflower sweater.

And when he expresses
something besides humor or anger,
you tell him to open up more often—
never demanding him to “man up.”

And when he tells you that
others hate him without knowing him,
you pick up your sword
and join his fight—
because he is your son.

Catching Dragon, Part 4

It's surprising the neighbors haven't complained
about a full-grown dragon in our backyard.

Not once in the past year has anyone mentioned
how loudly he rumbles when hungry—
or why, despite his velvet-purple wings,
he chooses to stay grounded.

No matter how much we encouraged him,
he refused to fly.
We tried to get him to flap his wings,
but he'd only turn his head to the sky, frowning,
before picking up a deflated soccer ball in his jaws
and dropping it at my youngest daughter's feet.

I worried—what kind of dragon wouldn't want to fly?
But every time I asked, my daughter would shush me,
kiss his scaly cheek, and say,
Look how beautiful.

June Wedding

We walk down the aisle together—
I glide in lace, my daughter's hand
damp in mine.
Her little feet stumble in stiff dress shoes,
and my nervous legs tremble,
but we manage to stay upright.
We have always held each other up.

At the aisle's end waits a man—
the one who will be my husband,
her father—by choice.
A man who has let his roots grow deep,
intertwining them with my daughter's life,
a daughter who has waited so patiently
to be loved by a father.

My daughter's cotton dress brushes
against my hem as she lets go of my hand—
then runs. Arms outstretched,
she reaches for her father,
a father who, this time, reaches back,
lifts her high, spinning—
an oak with a tire swing swaying.

Stepfather's Song

I'm blessed,
but a false father
once looked at my sapling
and called her firewood.

Little sapling withered,
couldn't stand straight
learned to reject sunlight.
Until.

I sang warmth
hushed sadness
nurtured self-love

And now we both stretch skyward.

More Than Anything

If she becomes a
doctor—beautiful
teacher—wonderful
electrician—so clever
waitress—hardworking
police officer—so brave
(insert job here)—incredible,

I would be proud of whatever
she grows to be.

But more than anything,
I always want her honey eyes
sparking when lightning cracks,
wolf mind resilient
while facing fire,
and a chest full of kindness
when freeing lost ants
from the kitchen to the outdoors.

Mama Bear

I never understood the term "mama bear" until a child flicked my daughter on the head and suddenly I was strong as 12 lumberjacks, puma fast, agile as a raccoon on meth, with a grizzly growl bold enough to scare even the blood thirstiest away. Luckily for that kid my daughter gave him a righteous face slap and he ran disappearing into the sea of children on the jungle gym. But I can't have my daughter slapping others, so I showed her how to properly throw a punch. *The power comes from your core, throw shoulder, and hips, but most importantly don't forget your fire heart.* My baby will be fine, but I'll sharpen my claws just in case.

Snapdragon

My daughter and I are
forever linked by ancient
magic of a mother's bond.

Veins are intertwined
fates etched into bone
Our roots are the same.
They wind around each other,
as if you can't tell one from the other.
We hold each other upright.

I've noticed she's been expanding.
Still holding on to my roots,
but stretching new ones
through the damp cool earth.
I wonder what she'll find.

My flora is a rose,
representing, love, passion, and friendship.
The earth is made of mostly roses.
But hers isn't tame like a rose,
She's something
of a more vibrant species.
I'll always protect her petals.

Should evil seek her.
I'll send her away on the backs of owls
piloting through night's sky,

stars like dazzling lilies
floating upon an inky pond.

Athena will embrace her.
She has always known my child.
Place a crown of cream blossoms on her head.
Taken from her olive tree in full bloom.
I will face the turmoil.

Because I'm her exhausted
slightly dented shield;
one day she will
become a sword.

Until then,
I'll patiently wait to see if her heart
ever turns into a common rose
and pray to every god
imaginable that hers will always
remain a snapdragon.

Pushing through rocks and thistle and glass.
Only drinking wild rain
and eating the land's nutrients.
Inspired by bravery, courage, and the promise of macaroni
for lunch.

Power Not Powder

My daughter comes from a line
of proud women
resilience draped
gemmed in persistence
grit born—fueling fire
calloused feet bare—
foundation in power
not powder
strong body
stronger mind
iron boned
honey
hearted
soul.

Those with Daughters

I hope when she cusses,
you don't tell her to be a lady,
but laugh because she learned it from you.

and when she chooses "boy clothes"
instead of pink frills,
you tell her she looks amazing in that red truck shirt.

and when she is strong, when she is fierce,
you tell her to lean into it—not quiet down.

and when she refuses the damsel's role,
choosing instead to be the hero,
you remember how capable she is, so you give her
armor, swords, and a promise she can always come home.

Milestones

When the day's mistakes feel too heavy,
when parenthood seems impossible, something you can't handle.

Remind yourself: you grew an entire human being—
nervous system, organs, personality and all.

And remember how, at midnight,
one day transforms into the next—giving you a chance to reset.

Bad days aren't who you are,
and you too will reach milestones.

Catching Dragon, Part 5

After days of rain
I kicked my kids outside to play.

Where our napping dragon
rolled on his back.
I could hear him sigh like muted thunder rolling in.

I heard sweet shouting
and looked out to find my kids
on the dragon's claws
doing yoga.

One in pigeon pose
another, palm tree
and the last, impressively in crow.

The dragon snored making them
all lose their balance and fall
laughing.

I then went outside to show them how
to properly balance on their heads.

About the Author

Hannah Seelman lives in southwest Michigan with her husband, three-year-old daughter, and two chaotic dogs. She is a student at Western Michigan University, where she is earning an MFA in both poetry and teaching writing composition.

She's active in the creative writing community running workshops, giving readings, and volunteering for *Third Coast Magazine.* Although she loves her work, her favorite time of day is when she can simply read a book with a dog sleeping on her lap while her husband makes his incredibly delicious burritos. Her poetry is published in *Ink Nest Poetry, Thistle Magazine, Feminist Wire,* and was a Finalist for Dreamer Poetry competition spring 2025.

Instagram:
hannah_e_seelman

www.ingramcontent.com/pod-product-compliance
Lightning Source LLC
LaVergne TN
LVHW090616110826
845146LV00001B/420

* 9 7 9 8 9 0 1 4 6 8 1 3 5 *